Snippets From a Busy Mind

BY

Karyn Finneron

Published in the United States and the United Kingdom

ISBN 978-0-9857362-8-6

First edition 2023

Printed in the United States of America

Acknowledgments

Thanks to my family, friends and Writers Group members for their inspiration and thoughts and support. Thanks to my friend, Elisabeth Cotton for her assistance with editing and always being available to help me.

A special thanks to my granddaughter Isabella for her illustrations and cover design. I have so enjoyed doing this project with her. The generational differences and ideas have blended well together.

I COME TO THE WATER

I come to the water to heal my soul
I come to the water for peace
I come to the water and then I hear
Your voice calming my soul

Sometimes I feel so lost and alone
Sometimes I can't find my way
I try to fix things all on my own
But I only get in my way

I come to the water to heal my soul
I come to the water for peace
I come to the water and then I hear
Your voice calming my soul

My mind races so fast it hurts
My heart pounds like a drum
If I take a minute just to stop
I can wait for this fear to pass

I can go to the water and heal my soul
I can go to the water for peace
You will be waiting at the water for me
With your voice that can calm my soul

Father Sky Speaks to Mother Earth

"The Earth is ravaged," he said.
"I know," she replied.
"But we remember when it was green and beautiful."
"Yes", he stated,
"Green and beautiful, with all the colors of the earth and sky."
"They took it from us," she said.
"In the name of greed and progress, and we watched."
"Yes," he said.
"They stuffed their pockets while they stuffed
the people's ears with lies."
"They did," she said.
"Now, when they cannot turn back,
they try to fill the rivers with their tears."
"Yes," he said.
"But tears do little to heal the wounds they have caused."
"Foolish people with selfish hearts cripple the land and the bounty
that was given."
She looked at him with tears falling on dry cheeks.
"My children have ruined my gifts forever."

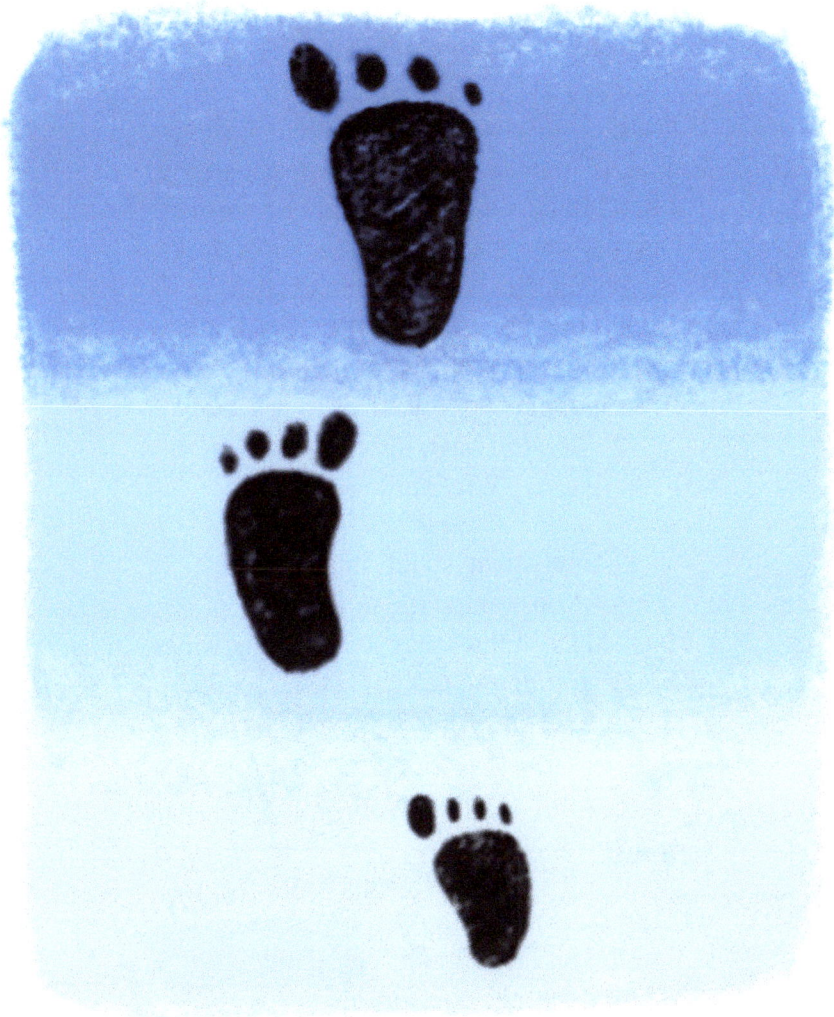

FOOTSTEPS

My feet are moving down this road,
The road you gave me long ago.
It was Your gift, this road called, "Life."
I remember when my foot steps were strong,
When I believed nothing could go wrong.
Along the way, there were side tracks, forks,
Things that forced me to choose.
I know You put them there to make me who I am,
And sometimes I chose well, but sometimes I went wrong.
Sometimes I felt alone and looked up to ask You, "WHY?"
"Why do I have to be strong?"
"Why am I so
weak?"
So many "whys" left unanswered
You wanted me to learn,
You said that I must stay and find my way.
Now I'm on the last part of the road,
I don't know how much further I will go,
But this much I have learned,
In the times that were most difficult,
The times filled with dread,
If I just took a moment,
stopped, and bowed my head,
I could feel you in the silence,
I could feel the comfort in your voice.
When it is time, Lord, will I know?
Will I see the bright light of which they speak?
Will it be Your hand that reaches out to guide my way?
I'm counting on Your promise, Lord,
The one I heard you speak

"Come to Me all you who have labored, and I will give you rest."
I hope you understand I always tried my best.
And when that day comes will I look in Your face and see,
You, smiling, arms open wide, waiting to welcome me?

GENTLE MILE

I will walk a gentle mile with Thee
And my heart will be burden free
For I will take myself down to the sea
And I will walk a gentle mile with Thee
My heart is heavy with fear
I can no longer feel you near
But I will go again to the sea
And there I will walk a gentle mile with Thee
My time with You makes me free
From my troubles and my grief
I feel my heart unburdened be
As I walk that gentle mile with Thee
Somehow the troubles that so burdened me
Lift off my shoulders when by the sea
My heavy heart now beats free
Because I walked that gentle mile with Thee.

JESUS, DID YOU KNOW?

Jesus, did you know, did you see?
They took us from our homes
In your name, Jesus.
They ripped us from our mothers' arms.
Did you see and hear what they did
While saying it was for You?
Jesus, did you know they stole our souls?
In your name they took us from our land.
Did you see how they changed us, hurt us
In ways too horrible to say?
Did you know, Jesus?
They told us that you loved us
That you were the Lord of love and hope.
Did you know they emptied us, in your name?
Did you know?
DID YOU?

Author's Note: Written in response to the treatment of Canada's First
Nation people by the priests and sisters from France.

FEELING HURT

How many times can someone be hurt?
Countless times,
How many times can someone be forgiven?
Someone, in the Good Book, asked.
"Seventy times?"
"No, seventy times seven," was the response.
"Why?" I wonder.
But, I've no one to ask.
I ponder, turning it over in my head.
The answer isn't there.

My eyes well up,
Somewhere inside, I hear a voice
"It's in your heart, not your head."
"Your pride and ego can't forgive."
"Listen to your soul."
"Listen to the whisper."
"It is I,"
Softly saying, 'Be at peace,
Love alone is the way to forgive.'
I close my eyes,
I give in to the truth.

HAVE YOU EVER

Have you ever been so angry, you could just scream?
Been full of rage, thrown things just to get a release;
Have you ever been so sad that you cried and ran out of tears?
Wanted to take your life, make a change or just lie down and die?
Have you ever been so tired of everything, wanted to give up?
Knew that you can't take another step, and yet you did.

Have you ever been so happy that you thought life was perfect?
Your heart and soul took flight.
Have you ever been left without the faith to believe it will get better?
Have you ever been so hopeful, believed that God, Yaweh, Allah,
the Great Spirit, the Universe, would help you through?

Have you ever been so in love with life, yourself,
someone, anyone, anything that
Gave your life purpose and meaning.
Did you ever ask yourself?

"Have I ever…"

LOOKING FOR FALL

Where oh where is fall?
It is September after all.
I know the dread of what comes after,
It can make us fear one leaf's fall.
But I am ready for
All that fall holds in store.
Warm days, cool nights,
Apples, pumpkins are a hearts delight.
Sweaters, piles of leaves,
A warm fire and cinnamon tea,
Oh what a treasure it all will be.
I keep searching for one colored leaf
So I can see the fall begin
But summer seems not to let it in.
Patient I must be,
Hoping that fall is waiting, also, for me

CHRISTMAS WARMTH

"It is here again," she said to him,
"The happiest season of all."
Funny, she didn't feel so happy,
No, not at all.
"The world's a mess, so much sadness all around."
"I wish I could go back
To our Christmases long past."
Everyone seemed so much happier,
Even though we never had a lot."
Her thoughts seemed to get much sadder,
She could hear a tear drop – plop.
"We're not alone, there's you and me," said he
A full house was what she needed.
So off to the phone, a text, a call,
Some said, "no" but more said "yes"
Now to put herself to the test.
She scurried back and forth
From cupboard to the pan
Before you knew it,
It was as if it had been planned
He just shook his head,
"Whatever makes her happy," is what he said
The doorbell rang, friends and family arrived.
"Such a nice idea," they said
A holiday "come as you are."
She stepped back from the crowd, felt all warm inside
And just for a minute she thought she felt
Those who had passed, by her side.
She turned and he was there
A big smile spread wide

"Reminds you of the Christmases past," he whispered.
For just a moment he felt it too;
The love of all their holidays before
And all the memories they had stored.

Holidays

This is the season for
Giving thanks, not playing pranks
Spending time and spending dimes
Taking time to pause,
Reflect,
On what is the reason for the season
It can be to celebrate the feast of lights
Or to honor the birth of the special child
Perhaps Kwanzaa may be your reason celebrating
Or maybe it is the green circle of holly wreaths
Druids gave them, believing in the magic of the season
Romans hung them on doors as a sign of victory
Whatever you choose to believe,
Just believe it is a special time to enjoy, live, laugh
But most of all take time to love

FATHER'S DAY

Out come the old pictures
I smile at my dad and me.
Him smiling young and strong
Me, the little girl in his arms,
The pictures tell the story of a dad.
The years roll by and he becomes
An older dear, granddad

Another photo shows my family.
My husband, cherished dad.
I look at the pictures of him,
Holding baby number one
Then, two and three.
Each one different,
Special in their way.
These pictures are a story,
Capture treasured times

The next chapter of his life,
A grampy now himself,
Pictures of him with beaming grandchildren.
Where did the time go?
So many years,
Countless Fathers' Days,
Remembered with smiles
And happy tears.

HEART SOUNDS

You know them, the soft ones of a regular beat
You hear them when your soul feels deep
There are the flutters, the skips
The ones that you know are going to hurt
There are some that make you want to sing
Some that make you want to melt
Some that make you scream and rage
And some that you wish you never felt
Heart sounds,
Listen, feel, and hear
Without them we are nothing.
We just disappear

ANOTHER BIRTHDAY

We knew seventy was on the way,
"I have no goals for it," you say.
Eighteen found high school complete,
Twenty-one you discovered beer was a treat.
At twenty-two you did not tarry,
Your sweet girl you asked to marry.
Thirty no longer young.
But three little ones still provided fun.
Forty found you admitting, you were bald,
And that left you somewhat appalled.
Looking around at fifty
An emptying nest seemed nifty
Now there was more time for both of you
Retired at sixty with lots to do
Travel, golf, me and you
Now look at you, seventy you did reach
What, is the goal, for this high peak?
"It means I get a break you see,
The goal is to play from the senior tee!"

GOLDEN YEARS

I pick up my bag of fears, years and tears
Off I go down the path of the "Golden Years."
I feel sorry for my self – being old
But, not long on the path, I see another, old and lonely
That's not me!
Off I go again and see someone old and infirm
They are frail, wasted and weak.
I pause, I cry and then hurry by
That's not me!
My bag of fears, years and tears seems less weighted now;
I walk the path again,
But soon I see old, confused, lost, unknown
"Please NO!" I cry as I hurry by
Again, that's not me.
I take a rest, sit in the sun
Think on my life, long past begun.
I'm looking at my bag of fears, years and tears
Thinking of all I tucked inside;
While walking the path of my "Golden Years"
I realize,
There in that bag is more joy than tears,
More happiness than fears.
I pick up my bag and continue on
Wondering what's left of the "Golden Years."

LIFE

How do you look back
On a life
What were the accomplishments
What was created
Education
Career
Love
Family
Relationships
Money
Fame
Did it all come from me
Did my best self-shine through
Did I go inside
To seek
To find
Myself and others
Or did the way get lost
In silly stumbles
Did the seeking go on
Because the life still
Lies incomplete

I AM

The writer who cannot write
The speaker who cannot speak
I wander lost, not found
Where am I going
Just circling round and round
I was a dreamer who never lived the dream
The reaper with no more to sow

Where will this journey take me
What will be the end
Sadly, I may not know

CAROUSEL

Sitting and watching children and horses fly by
I become transfixed by the music.
I see people enjoying the summer day.
Misty eyes take over, and I wane nostalgic.
I'm thinking of how I loved that magical ride.
I can remember my hair blowing free, as upon my steed, I did fly.
Coming around full circle, I see my mom and dad smiling.
I smile and bravely wave my hand.
They are gone now but the carousel spins on.
Making more happy childhood memories
For all who will take the ride.

THREE LITTLE FACES

They look at me, but
They don't see me.
They are held in time,
A small photo, taken long ago.
Three little faces, now grown
Gone off to lives of their own
Some days, I just pass them by;
Other days, like today,
I pick them up
Kiss three little faces, and
Miss yesterday

HONKY TONK GIRL

I'm just a honky tonk girl
Setting off to see the world.
Striking off on my own,
Don't even need a home.

I got off that bus and looked around
At the place called Music Town,
With my guitar and dreams.
I'm just a honky tonk girl
Setting off to see the world.

I had my hopes, my dreams,
They lay unfulfilled, for a honky tonk girl,
In the music world.

The days turned into years.
I played,
I sang.
I poured my heart and soul
Into the honky tonk world.

One day the girl woke up to see,
A woman, staring back at me.
The honky tonk girl,
Now, she's lost in that music world.
No more honky tonk girl,
Just a woman in her place,

All that's left of that honky tonk girl
Is a memory with a woman's face.
I'm forever the honky tonk girl,
Setting off to see that music world.

GONE HOME

Who will weep for this woman?
What has been her life
She was not famous
She hung her head in shame
She held her head high in pride
She rose each day at the rising sun
She worked until her hands were raw
She birthed sons and daughters
Some she sent to war
Many went on to babies of their own
Some never saw the light of a bright new day
She loved, laughed, cried, sinned
Lived fully and died
Who will weep for this woman?
I will weep for her
Because she is a mother, gone home

CRAZY LOVE

"I love you," he said.
"I know," she said.
"You're crazy," he said.
"I know, but it is the kind of crazy
That wraps around your heart.
It makes you want to stay," she smiled.
"But, I'll stay, forever," he said.
"Ah, yes, you will, but will I?" she asked.
"Will You!" he pleaded.
"I'll see," she said.
"But if I leave,
Then, you'll know what crazy really is."

THE NARROW DOOR

Did you ever, for a minute, think of your life as narrow doors?
How did you get here?
Was it through the narrow door of the birth canal
or through a narrow incision?
What was the next door?
Learning to roll, crawl, sit, walk, talk.
Difficult doors to pass through, but on you went.
Next, was the door of learning, going to school, tying your shoes.
Did someone teach you how to read, pray, behave, write?
No matter how narrow the door, you found your way through.
Perhaps, one of the most difficult doors was the door to adulthood
Leaving childhood behind and taking that lonely walk
Toward college, service, work, marriage.
Each choice, a door to an unknown world, but necessary to open
Looking at the door of parenthood,
did you really want to squeeze on through?
Career, single, parent, which one was your narrow door?
Then the end was in sight, retirement, a job well done or just done.
Were you ready, anxious, joyous, excited?
Not too many doors left now a door to be
a grandparent, great grandparent?
When it comes down to the last narrow door,
will you look back and want more?
Or will you look back, see all the memories, smile, cry,
and go through
Remembering all those who helped you through the narrow door.

BOOKS

Love them or leave them they are special
They give us a taste of the world
It matters not if they are truth or fable
They can be historic or current events
Today they can even be pageless
A vision on a computer screen
But please not for me!
I much prefer the feel and turn of the page
You can get lost in the story
Or perhaps you can imagine yourself where it takes place
A good book can make you laugh, cry, learn, think
It can take you places you have never been
Inspire you to try new things
Help you begin or change a career
Ah books, I could go on,
but my latest adventure is calling
Au revoir! I learned that in a book too!
Books
Love them or leave them they are something special

IMAGINATION

Into the dark maw I go,
Reminds me of a cave I used to know,
The cave was dark and damp,
Made me wish I had taken a lamp.
The cavern is wet and loud.
I can see the giants coming down.
They run over me, up and down.
Spewing heat, and water all around
I close my eyes.
I don't like to see,
Those giant things, hammering at me.
At last I'm done. I see the light.
I proceed on into the bright.
Now my car is all fresh and new.
I'll just bet I was scaring you!

THE BLUES

Funny how feelings can just suddenly wash over you
Outside the sky is blue and the day sunshine bright
But the "blues" that come over me make me sad
Then I think about my life and what I had and lost
I really have no reason for the mood that I am in
I get stuck in soulful memories of how it used to be
I think of how I felt when everyone I loved was still alive
I can remember smiles and hugs of those who have gone on
And think of what I would give to spend just one more day
With grandparents, mom, dad, relatives and friends
My eyes fill up and my tears spill over
Then I come back from the memories
Life is not all perfect but most of it is good
And so I chase the blues away, for now
But I know when I am down, they will find their way to me again

YOU AND ME

Isn't it amazing,
Hard to believe it's true,
That of all the people in the world,
You found me, or did I find you?
What was it that made us say,
"I'd like to know you a bit more today."
Was it my smile or was it your laugh?
Maybe it is the way with people you act.
In any case, the tiny spark became a flame,
And before we knew it, I took your name.
We became one and off we went,
Not knowing what "together" really meant.
Now we look back and we can see
All the things we did formed a memory.
It may not be perfect,
There were bruises, bumps
Laughter, some tears,
But we made it work.
I helped you and you helped me,
And we became this family.
Love formed a bond
That lasted through the years.
I still think when I look at you,
"Isn't it amazing that you found me
And I found you?"

GHOSTS

Out fly the ghosts of a haunted past
I've hung on so long afraid
To set them free from what is me.
They cried out from within
Longing for freedom but…
I hushed them and made them mute.
Now after so long I can no longer close my ears
Their screams of rage from the darkness begged me,
"Set us free!"
Then I went into the depths of me
Opened a window long past shut
The ghosts flew out
The screaming stopped
What was left was the bright light of me
Only me

BUDDIES

We were buddies, we two
Walking to school just me and you.
Friends we would always be,
Walking through life, you and me.
Our school days were filled with fun;
Passing the girls oh how we'd run.
"Don't slow down!"
No "sissy" stuff for us,
Just being buddies, that was enough.
Remember when the times were rough?
Our folks out of work
No money for fun.
We jumped on the trolley
We had a free run.
Time marched on
School days were done.
Then came the war,
WWII
The Navy for me,
The Army for you.
We grew up then.
Suffered along, with so many men.
We came home but, lost touch
We made lives.
We got old.
One day the heavens aligned.
Two old buddies were assigned
To a facility that cares for the aged.
A kind person asks
"Would you like to meet another Vet?"
A quick response, "you bet!"

Into the room I go for a look.
Frank? Anthony?
Two old buddies together again
Because time can never diminish love for a friend

Author's note: This poem was written in honor of two WWII veterans. Frank, I knew and went to visit him in a nursing home. He brought me to meet Anthony. Two old friends re-connected. I had the pleasure of visiting them for two hours. The poem is the result of the visit.

ACCEPTANCE

The little boy stood puzzled and surprised
He watched the other boys at play eyes opened wide
He was trying hard to understand why all the boys at play
Did not invite a certain boy they all pushed away
"Come on," a boy yelled to him, "we have to go; let him stay."
"But why can't he come?" the boy inquired
"Oh, him, he's not like us; he's a bum,
We don't want him, no way!"
Left alone the boy was thinking,
"Come on, just let him play."
Another kid came by and it was just the same
"Come on, leave him, we'll miss the game."
"Wait!" said the boy. "Can you tell me why?"
"Can't we find some room for just one more guy?"
"No, can't you see, he's not like you and me."
"But he's a kid like us, why not?"
The other kid then ran off too; left him all alone.
Thinking of all that happened, he just let out a moan
His parents always taught him that people are the same
We may be different colors and have different names
"Just like the rainbow," his mom said,
"Even the flowers are yellow, blue and red
There are so many colors,
Clouds of white and skies and seas of different blues."
Dad had told him it was like that for people too
"Be kind, respect everyone,
And you will see what the world can become."
So the boy went over to the so called "bum"
Stretched out his hand and said, "Come."
Off they went to play and perhaps
To become friends one day

CRYING

I can hear the whimpers if I really listen
Who's crying
I look around and I see no one
Yet the whimpers become louder
As my day goes by I see
Horror, looking back at me
I watch the replay of the guns
I see the faces of people on the run
Once again, I hear whimpers now changed to sobs
It is America I hear crying
The sobs become louder as on my screen I see
Bloodied, beaten frightened people looking back at me
Next, I hear and see people screaming at each other
Telling lies, tearing flags, brother against brother
America, my country, my home
It seems as if you've nothing left but bones
It is America I hear sobbing
Can no one hear but me
America, America what happened
My country 'tis of thee

MEMORIES

I stand, looking out at the sea
Today for a reason unclear, I feel me
I feel my soul yearning, longing for   The me that used to be
I wanted to feel the beauty of the sea
Take it in; make it part of me   I put on the long, blue dress,   You
loved that dress
You said it matched the blue in my eyes
The blue I stole from the skies   Just as then,
I stand looking at the sea
Remembering when you came up behind me
Wrapped those forever warm arms around me
Just for a moment, I was the me
The me I wanted and was meant to be.
Now I look to the sea and I miss
The you and me that used to be

WHEN I AM GONE

The day will come when I am gone
A day they say I will go home
To a place promised long ago
A place I'm told I will know
But left behind you will be
Left alone and without me
Go to the places that we knew
All the lovely places I shared with you
Feel me in the breeze by the sea
Feel the sun that warmed you and me
Be silent, breathe in those places
I'm there silently in those spaces You will feel me
And then you may hear me
Listen to your heart
And know that only time keeps us apart